BOOK I

THE INSPIRATIONS OF WOLF

A WORKING JOURNAL FOR GROWTH
AND ADVANCED ESL LEARNERS

BY

WOLFGANG SCHIFER

 FriesenPress

Suite 300 - 990 Fort St
Victoria, BC, V8V 3K2
Canada

www.friesenpress.com

ISBN
978-1-5255-6538-0 (Hardcover)
978-1-5255-6539-7 (Paperback)
978-1-5255-6540-3 (eBook)

1. SELF-HELP, PERSONAL GROWTH

Distributed to the trade by The Ingram Book Company

MY NOTE TO YOU!

Welcome!

I want to extend a warm congratulations to you on this extraordinary new beginning by obtaining this book. Whether you've purchased, borrowed, or found this book, my intention is that it will, at the very least, help you feel more empowered than before you read it—that it will inspire you in some way; that it will help you grow, resolve, or understand a little bit more about yourself. By obtaining this book, you have taken the first step to a better outlook on life, and ultimately, a better you. Before you begin on your daily journey, allow me first to tell you how I came to write this book.

Once upon a time I lived in Colombia. I was there for approximately four years, teaching English at one of the top Universities in the city of Medellin. Wait, let me backup just a little bit more.

I was born and raised in a small town in Alberta, Canada called Fort McMurray. I was raised in a not-so-affluent part of the town, in a trailer park, in a city that was devoted to the mining sector. My options growing up poor were slim. Looking back at my younger years, my father inculcated valuable lessons in me that, for some reason or another, never really clicked until I was older. One lesson, however, that popped into my head time and time again was, "Be the best." He told me that if I became a janitor, be the best janitor I could be. No matter what job I had, I always tried to do my best, and to excel at everything I took on. Little did I know just how deeply ingrained those words were in me. I usually instinctively followed them. When I was about nineteen years of age, I began my first career. Growing up in a city where mining was pretty much the only option, I decided, after much struggle in life, to go into the trades. Trades paid well, and for other reasons I won't get into, I picked Heavy Duty Mechanics. This trade, although not something that was in my heart to do, taught me so much, and provided me with the capital to begin my second career.

I went into Real Estate at the age of twenty-one, and moved to Edmonton. My real estate career landed me a position with an investment company and in the crash of late 2007, I began planning my move to Colombia. I had made enough in my career to purchase a small condo there and felt it was time for something new and exciting.

Before moving to Colombia, I also worked as a Business Development Consultant for a couple of companies and then, at the age of twenty-five, I sold what I could, and made the leap—over six thousand km south—to one of the most beautiful cities in the world. Without a clue in the world, yet still thinking I knew it all, finally, Medellin was my new home. Being half Colombian, this was a place I always wanted to move to—so much that I even tried to convince my mother, when I was about sixteen, to move there. I even wrote up a contract with her, promising to be good if we left Canada for Colombia. Yeah, I guess business is in my blood. Who writes a contract at that age with their parents?

Anyway, the city of Medellin and its people stole my heart, literally, (as I eventually married my first wife there). With what I made in real estate, I bought a small condo and renovated it to my liking. I felt invigorated… and also a little lost. It didn't take long for me to figure out that, although in Canada I could wheel and deal, work in business with my experience, or at the very least pull wrenches and earn a very good living, Colombia demanded diplomas, which I, of course, did not have. I soon learned that getting a job was very difficult and I couldn't find decent work! Being twenty-five with loads of experience in different areas of business didn't matter, as everyone still demanded some sort of degree, and mechanics was not exactly something I wanted to do in that country.

I finally landed a job as a manager in an American company, and I quickly learned that ethics in that part of the world were not on par with what I was used to. The job only lasted two weeks, and then I was on the search again.

On the recommendation of my family, I decided to look into teaching. Teaching?! I didn't know anything about teaching, and understanding the local belief system—needing a diploma for anything and everything—teaching seemed out of bounds as well. However, to my surprise, I learned that I didn't need a teaching diploma. Being bilingual and holding dual citizenship helped with this, and I decided to take the lowest paying job I have ever taken in my life, to gain experience. Earning less than three dollars an hour, I began to teach.

I realized soon enough that I was not only loving it, but I was made for it. It became my passion. The instinctive, "Be your best," came through and I shone! My teaching methodology quickly spread, and to my delight, I was asked to work at the University of Medellin, where I consistently received top professor reputation and status. I soon began to teach private classes to high profile students.

It was the best time of my life. It was in these classes that I used my experience in life to have discussions, pose questions, and share thoughts and cultures with my students. At one point, one of my more dedicated and memorable students—Marta was her name—recommended that I write a book. Those words never left my mind. Eventually, it came time for me to return to Canada with my Colombian wife. The plan was to get her Canadian citizenship, save up, buy another Colombian property, and move back to start a family. I knew that the experience was going to be very difficult, and I had decided to use the time back in Canada to begin writing my first book. Marta's words echoed in my mind and I was dedicated to my goal.

During the course of my first year back in Canada, I wrote my first book, one I hope to publish as well in the future. It was quite the experience. Writing it helped me understand so much more about myself, and my potential. However, after writing the book, our marriage became increasingly unstable, and, over time, I transitioned into what would be some of the darkest moments in my life. Fortunately for me, the book I had written gave me strength and courage to understand that everything is cyclical, and I had to do whatever I could to climb out of this emotionally turbulent time.

This is where this book comes into play. You see, in order to cope and deal with much of what I went through, I went to the gym. A lot! Physical fitness for me is extremely important, and exercising allows me to meditate on my mind, body, and soul. When I'm in deep concentration, sweating, and in that state of mind, my mind opens up and begins to meditate on its own. I eventually started to write down these thoughts.

Originally, these moments of personal inspiration were intended for just myself, although I posted many of them on Facebook. I knew that after a year, Facebook would do me the kind favour of sending my positive memories back to me on my feed, and my own words would provide me random, and hopefully timely, courage, strength, and positivity. My present self was preparing for my future self, and my future self would be thankful to what would be my past self.

Interestingly, over time, random people on my Facebook began to send me positive feedback and even private messages, telling me how thankful they were for my posts. To any Educator/Teacher out there, you know that this is the best gift you can receive; knowing you have helped change someone's life for the better. This is what inspired me to compile all my thoughts and share them with you.

I hope that at least one person, reading this book at the appropriate time, will come across words of encouragement. I hope it will be at that moment that they will say to themselves, "this was exactly what I needed today." If only one person has a reaction like that, I will feel that this has been worth it. I know, for me, I have said that about my own words, and I am positive that others will feel the same.

When you read these daily words, I encourage you not to always take them at face value. These words were originally written for me, and they have deeper meaning than is immediately obvious on the surface. And they could mean something entirely different for you, at the given moment, than they did for me, or that they will for any other person. I implore you to read these words, and take your time to analyse them throughout the day. See how they fit into your personal life for that day, and how you can apply them. Or think about how they could work in your life in the future.

Think about what you can extract from them for your own personal benefit, and for your own growth. I have experienced sharing these words with others at the most random times to share encouragement. During these moments, when I least expected it, I would recall a quote, and insert it into a conversation at what seemed to be just the right occasion for the other party.

If this book touches you in any way, I suggest that you pay it forward to help another person with these words. You never know how you can change someone's life for the better just by being there, listening, or sharing information. I truly do hope that my journey through my own personal path and growth may serve to help you along yours.

Additionally, this book can serve as a tool for all my fellow English teachers out there. This book provides a daily dosage of English words and conversational pieces to use with your students. You will be able to describe new words to them, show how it translates into context, and create a dialogue with your learner about how they interpret each day's words. Tell them to write down their thoughts in English on the page provided and you can review with them their grammar, use of vocabulary, and structure. Allowing them to express how they feel about each passage will provide a great way to convey their ideas, and practice daily communication skills. I can't help but think that this will be a fun, encouraging, and interactive learning resource for English learners. Whether you are studying English for yourself, you are an educator or just a lifelong learner, I encourage you to write your thoughts on the page provided for each day, and how you took my inspiration and made it your own experience. The important part is that you make this book your own!

Before you begin, I will leave you with this last note. In business, people leverage all the time. You can also leverage in life. I would like to leverage my experiences for you. From the bottom of my heart, I hope you become a better person because of it. That is my purpose. So, thank you for purchasing this book, and remember that these words are just one ingredient. Feed your mind, body, and soul all things healthy! Enjoy!

LIBRO I

LAS INSPIRACIONES DE WOLF

UN DIARIO DE TRABAJO PARA EL
CRECIMIENTO Y LOS ESTUDIANTES
AVANZADOS DE ESL

POR

WOLFGANG SCHIFER

¡UNA NOTA PARA TODOS!

¡Bienvenidos!

Quiero felicitarles cordialmente por este nuevo y extraordinario comienzo al obtener este libro. Ya sea que hayas comprado, prestado o encontrado este libro, mi intención es que, como mínimo, te ayude a sentirte más poderoso que antes de leerlo; que te inspire de alguna manera; que te ayude a crecer, a resolver o a entender un poco más sobre ti mismo. Al obtener este libro, usted ha dado el primer paso hacia una mejor perspectiva de la vida y, en última instancia, hacia un mejor usted. Antes de que empiece su viaje diario, permítame primero decirle cómo llegué a escribir este libro.

Hace mucho tiempo viví en Colombia. Estuve allí aproximadamente cuatro años, enseñando inglés en una de las mejores universidades de la ciudad de Medellín. Espere, déjeme retroceder un poco más.

Nací y me crie en un pequeño pueblo de Alberta, Canadá, llamado Fort McMurray. Me crie en una parte no tan próspera de la ciudad, en un parque de casas rodantes, en una ciudad que se dedicaba al sector minero. Mis opciones al crecer en la pobreza eran escasas. Mirando hacia atrás a mis años de juventud, mi padre me inculcó valiosas lecciones que, por alguna razón u otra, nunca me hicieron efecto hasta que fui mayor. Una lección, sin embargo, que me vino a la mente una y otra vez fue: "Sé el mejor". Me dijo que, si me convertía en conserje, debería ser el mejor conserje que pudiera existir. No importaba el trabajo que tuviera que hacer, que siempre trataba de hacer lo mejor posible y de sobresalir en todo lo que emprendía. No sabía lo profundamente arraigadas que estaban esas palabras en mí. Por lo general, las seguía instintivamente. Cuando tenía alrededor de diecinueve años de edad, comencé mi primera carrera. Al crecer en una ciudad donde la minería era prácticamente la única opción, decidí, después de mucha lucha en la vida, dedicarme a los oficios técnicos. Los oficios técnicos pagaban bien, y por otras razones , que no entraré a explicar aquí, elegí la Mecánica de Trabajo Pesado. Este oficio, aunque no era algo que estuviera en mi corazón hacer, me enseñó mucho, y me proporcionó el capital para comenzar mi segunda carrera.

Entré en el sector inmobiliario a los veintiún años y me mudé a Edmonton. Mi carrera en bienes raíces me llevó a una posición en una compañía de inversión y en la crisis de finales de 2007, empecé a planear mi mudanza a Colombia. Ya había ganado lo suficiente en mi carrera como para comprar un pequeño condominio allí y sentí que era hora de algo nuevo y emocionante.

Antes de mudarme a Colombia, también trabajé como Consultor de Desarrollo de Negocios para un par de compañías y luego, a la edad de veinticinco años, vendí lo que pude, y di el salto—más de seis mil kilómetros al sur—a una de las ciudades más hermosas del mundo. Sin una sola pista del mundo, pero aun pensando que lo sabía todo, finalmente convertí a Medellín en mi nuevo hogar. Siendo mitad colombiano, este era un lugar al que siempre quise mudarme, tanto que incluso traté de convencer a mi madre, cuando tenía unos dieciséis años, de que se mudara allí. Incluso escribí un contrato con ella, prometiendo que sería bueno, si dejábamos Canadá irnos para ir a Colombia. Sí, supongo que el negocio está en mi sangre. ¿Quién escribe un contrato a esa edad con sus padres?

De todas maneras, la ciudad de Medellín y su gente me robaron el corazón, literalmente, (ya que eventualmente me casé con mi primera esposa allí). Con lo que hice en bienes raíces, compré un pequeño condominio y lo renové a mi gusto. Me sentí vigorizado... y también un poco perdido. No me tomó mucho tiempo darme cuenta de que, aunque en Canadá podía hacer negocios con mi experiencia, ganarme la vida muy bien, Colombia exigía diplomas, que yo, por supuesto, no tenía. ¡Pronto aprendí que conseguir un trabajo era muy difícil y que no podía encontrar un trabajo decente! Tener veinticinco años y mucha experiencia en diferentes áreas de negocios no importaba, ya que todo el mundo exigía algún tipo de título, y la mecánica no era exactamente algo que yo quería hacer en ese país.

Finalmente conseguí un trabajo como gerente en una empresa americana, y rápidamente aprendí que la ética en esa parte del mundo no estaba a la par con lo que yo estaba acostumbrado. El trabajo sólo duró dos semanas, y luego estuve en la búsqueda de uno nuevo.

Por recomendación de mi familia, decidí investigar sobre la enseñanza. ¡¿Enseñar?! No sabía nada sobre enseñanza, y al entender el sistema de creencias local—que un diploma era necesario para todo y para cualquier cosa- enseñar también parecía estar fuera de los límites. Sin embargo, para mi sorpresa, me enteré de que no necesitaba un diploma de enseñanza. Ser bilingüe y tener doble ciudadanía me ayudó con esto, y decidí tomar el trabajo de más bajo salario que he tomado en mi vida, para ganar experiencia. Ganando menos de tres dólares por hora, empecé a enseñar.

Pronto me di cuenta de que no sólo me encantaba, sino que estaba hecho para ello. Se convirtió en mi pasión. La expresión, *"Sé lo mejor que puedas", me llegó al alma, ¡y yo brillé!* Mi metodología de enseñanza se extendió rápidamente y, para mi deleite, me pidieron que trabajara en la Universidad de Medellín, donde constantemente me gané la mejor reputación y estatus de profesor. Pronto empecé a dar clases particulares a estudiantes de alto nivel.

Fue la mejor época de mi vida. Fue en estas clases que usé mi experiencia en la vida para tener discusiones, hacer preguntas, y compartir pensamientos y culturas con mis estudiantes. En un momento dado, una de mis estudiantes más dedicadas y memorables -Marta era su nombre- me recomendó que escribiera un libro. Esas palabras nunca salieron de mi mente. Eventualmente, llegó el momento de regresar a Canadá con mi esposa colombiana. El plan era obtener su ciudadanía canadiense, ahorrar, comprar otra propiedad colombiana y regresar para formar una familia. Sabía que la experiencia iba a ser muy difícil, y había decidido usar el tiempo de regreso a Canadá para empezar a escribir mi primer libro. Las palabras de Marta resonaron en mi mente y me dediqué a cumplir esa meta.

Durante el curso de mi primer año de regreso a Canadá, escribí mi primer libro, uno que espero publicar también en el futuro. Fue toda una experiencia. Escribirlo me ayudó a entender mucho más sobre mí misma y mi potencial. Sin embargo, después de escribir el libro, nuestro matrimonio se volvió cada vez más inestable y, con el tiempo, se convirtió en lo que serían algunos de los momentos más oscuros de mi vida. Afortunadamente para mí, el libro que había escrito me dio la fuerza y el coraje para entender que todo es cíclico, y tuve que hacer todo lo posible para salir de este tiempo emocionalmente turbulento.

Aquí es donde este libro entra en juego. Verán, para poder enfrentar y lidiar con mucho de lo que pasé, fui al gimnasio. Mucho. La condición física para mí es extremadamente importante, y el ejercicio me permite meditar en mi mente, cuerpo y alma. Cuando estoy en profunda concentración, sudando, y en ese estado mental, mi mente se abre y comienza a meditar por sí misma. Finalmente empecé a escribir estos pensamientos.

Originalmente, estos momentos de inspiración personal estaban destinados sólo para mí, aunque publiqué muchos de ellos en Facebook. Sabía que después de un año, Facebook me haría el amable favor de enviarme mis recuerdos positivos en un "Feed", y mis propias palabras me proporcionarían oportunamente, coraje, fuerza y positividad. Mi yo presente se estaba preparando para mi yo futuro, y mi yo futuro estaría agradecido a lo que sería mi yo pasado.

Curiosamente, con el tiempo, personas al azar en mi Facebook comenzaron a enviarme comentarios positivos e incluso mensajes privados, diciéndome lo agradecidos que estaban por mis publicaciones. Para cualquier educador o maestro, te das cuenta que este es el mejor regalo que puedes recibir; saber que has ayudado a cambiar la vida de alguien para mejor. Esto es lo que me inspiró a recopilar todos mis pensamientos y compartirlos con ustedes.

Espero que por lo menos una persona, al leer este libro en el momento apropiado, encuentre palabras de aliento. Espero que sea en ese momento cuando se digan a sí mismos, "esto era exactamente lo que necesitaba hoy". Si sólo una persona tiene una reacción así, sentiré que esto ha valido la pena. Yo sé que he dicho esto en relación a mis propias palabras, y estoy seguro de que otros sentirán lo mismo.

Cuando leas estas palabras diarias, te animo a que no las tomes siempre al pie de la letra. Estas palabras fueron escritas originalmente para mí, y tienen un significado más profundo de lo que es inmediatamente obvio en la superficie. Y en un momento dado, pueden significar algo completamente diferente para ti, de lo que significaron para mí, o de lo que significarán para cualquier otra persona. Te ruego que lea estas palabras, y que se tome su tiempo para analizarlas a lo largo del día. Vea cómo encajan en su vida personal ese día, y cómo puedes aplicarlas. O piensa en cómo podrían funcionar en tu vida en el futuro.

Piense en qué que puedes extraer de ellos muchas cosas para su propio beneficio personal y para su propio crecimiento. En los momentos más fortuitos he compartido estas palabras con otros con el fin de dales aliento. En esos momentos, cuando parecía ser la ocasión adecuada para la otra parte y cuando menos lo esperaba, recordaba una cita y la introducía en una conversación.

Si este libro te conmueve de alguna manera, te sugiero que lo compartas a fin de ayudar a otra persona con estas palabras. Nunca se sabe cómo se puede cambiar la vida de alguien para mejor con sólo estar ahí, escuchando o compartiendo información. Realmente espero que mi viaje a través de mi propio camino personal y crecimiento sirva para ayudarte a lo largo del tuyo.

Este libro puede servir, además, como una herramienta para todos mis compañeros profesores de inglés ya que proporciona una dosis diaria de vocabulario en inglés y piezas de conversación para usar con sus estudiantes. Usted podrá describirles las palabras nuevas, mostrarles cómo se traducen en cada contexto y crear diálogos con sus estudiantes sobre cómo interpretan las palabras de cada día. Dígales que escriban sus pensamientos en inglés en la página proporcionada y usted podrá revisar con ellos su gramática, uso de vocabulario y estructura. Permitiéndoles expresar cómo se sienten sobre cada pasaje les proporcionará una gran manera de transmitir sus ideas, y practicar las habilidades de comunicación diarias. No puedo evitar pensar que este será un recurso de aprendizaje divertido, alentador e interactivo para los estudiantes de inglés. Ya sea que estés estudiando inglés por ti mismo, o seas un educador o simplemente un aprendiz de por vida, te animo a que escribas tus pensamientos en la página proporcionada para cada día, y cómo te inspiraste en mí, y como lo convertiste en tu propia experiencia. *¡Lo importante es que hagas tuyo este libro!*

Antes de que empiece, le dejaré con esta última nota. En los negocios, la gente aprovecha su poder para influenciar otras personas. Este libro también se puede utilizar para influenciar a otras personas positivamente en asuntos de nuestras vidas. Me gustaría aprovechar mis experiencias para usted. Desde el fondo de mi corazón, espero que te conviertas en una mejor persona gracias a ello. Ese es mi propósito. Así que, gracias por comprar este libro, y recuerda que estas palabras son sólo un ingrediente. *¡Alimenta tu mente, cuerpo y alma con todas las cosas saludables! Disfrútelo!*

Wolfgang Schifer

IT BEGINS

DAY 1

"Vision is important, but to envision is imperative."

_____

_____

_____

_____

_____

_____

_____

_____

DAY 2

"We all need a little rescuing at one time or another. Do not dismiss an unexpected hero."

DAY 3

"Learn the skill and humility to absorb the greater truth."

_____

_____

_____

_____

_____

_____

_____

_____

DAY 4

"Listen for the natural screams for progression from your body and mind. Be in tune and stay in tune."

_____

_____

_____

_____

_____

_____

_____

_____

DAY 5

"Learn to follow the law of your inner instinct of probability."

DAY 6

"No one can climb a mountain in one leap. You get there by starting small. Plan ahead, start small, grow to leaps and bounds, and maintain momentum."

DAY 7

*"Condition yourself to the rewards of
achievements, and carry the lessons forward."*

_____

_____

_____

_____

_____

_____

_____

_____

DAY 8

"You should never fear knowledge that may shake the foundation on which your current belief system rests. On the contrary, you should search it out, question, and prove your beliefs true, or adapt to the greater truth. Never shy away from an opportunity to grow."

_____

_____

_____

_____

_____

_____

_____

_____

DAY 9

*"Pull up those who reach up. Likewise reach up
and search to be pulled up. It is futile to reach
for someone who refuses to be lifted up."*

_____

_____

_____

_____

_____

_____

_____

_____

DAY 10

"You are your own inspiration, you are your own motivation, you are your own success, and your own passion. It always has been, always will be, you, up to you, for you, and because of you."

_____

_____

_____

_____

_____

_____

_____

_____

DAY 11

"There is an epidemic of people becoming severely infected with the necessity of portraying themselves for the world to see on social media. Limiting and balancing it has become almost nonexistent in our day. Perhaps trying to exercise some privacy would do the soul good for those who have withheld themselves from it for so long."

_____

_____

_____

_____

_____

_____

_____

_____

_____

DAY 12

"Do not allow yourself to be unnecessarily affected when you have the power and the means to maintain your needs and wants."

_____

_____

_____

_____

_____

_____

_____

_____

DAY 13

"As things in life get harder, your willpower, drive, and determination must also increase in strength. How can you expect things to be easy when you remain the same, and everything else changes? Adapt to overcome."

DAY 14

"You must first be able to discern what is negative and evil before you can reject it. Once you reject it the first time, it becomes easier to reject it the second time. But remember, the potential strength of future negative/evil energy also increases."

_____

_____

_____

_____

_____

_____

_____

_____

DAY 15

"Sometimes the hardest thing to do is determining when to slow down and when to speed up, with accuracy."

_____

_____

_____

_____

_____

_____

_____

_____

DAY 16

"There are times when the wrong path may lead you to the right place. Don't shy away from trekking down an unbeaten path."

_____

_____

_____

_____

_____

_____

_____

_____

_____

DAY 17

"Concentrate your efforts on attaining the unattainable, and the journey will teach you more than you can ever imagine."

DAY 18

"Don't be a 'used to be.' Become an 'I am,' and an 'I will become.'"

_____

_____

_____

_____

_____

_____

_____

_____

DAY 19

"Do not be subdued by ignorance, hate, jealousy, fear, and all things wicked."

_____

_____

_____

_____

_____

_____

_____

_____

DAY 20

"Our bodies are not invincible, but our minds can be."

_____

_____

_____

_____

_____

_____

_____

_____

DAY 21

———

"You can't inspire others if you can't inspire yourself."

_____

_____

_____

_____

_____

_____

_____

_____

DAY 22

"We have more energy than we give ourselves credit for. Just dig for it."

DAY 23

"We are all fortunate in our own ways."

DAY 24

"Treat your mind, body, and soul as a business. The younger you are when you begin to invest in it, the more profitable it will become for you as you age."

DAY 25

"Be free to protect, to grow, and to
sustain your natural entirety."

_____

_____

_____

_____

_____

_____

_____

_____

DAY 26

"Who is the operator of a vehicle? A person.
Who is the operator of your body? Your mind.
Who is the operator of your mind? Your soul.
And how do you nourish your soul?"

_____

_____

_____

_____

_____

_____

_____

_____

DAY 27

"Discover your natural self, away from all the clutter and static that the media and other negative forces impose on you daily."

_____

_____

_____

_____

_____

_____

_____

_____

DAY 28

"ALLOW yourself to be happy, and become purposeful."

_____

_____

_____

_____

_____

_____

_____

_____

DAY 29

"Pain? Sweat it out! Pleasure?! Keep it up with sweat and sun!"

_____

_____

_____

_____

_____

_____

_____

_____

_____

DAY 30

"It is only gradually that bad habits form. However, it is exactly the same for good habits. Be aware of your habits!"

_____

_____

_____

_____

_____

_____

_____

_____

DAY 31

"In all categories of life, find out your minimum and your maximum, and balance accordingly. Always raise the bar. Always seek to adjust for the better."

DAY 32

*"Discipline doesn't just appear. It is yearned
for, cultivated, worked for, desired, and
attainable for those who practice it."*

_____

_____

_____

_____

_____

_____

_____

_____

DAY 33

"Fine tune the tunable, leverage the unchangeable, maximize the potential."

_____

_____

_____

_____

_____

_____

_____

_____

_____

DAY 34

"Search for ways you can use entropy as an advantage."

_____

_____

_____

_____

_____

_____

_____

_____

DAY 35

"Create an addiction to achieving."

_____

_____

_____

_____

_____

_____

_____

_____

DAY 36

"Step 1 – Create goals.
Step 2 – Push through them.
Step 3 – Repeat."

_____

_____

_____

_____

_____

_____

_____

_____

DAY 37

"Before you can soldier for someone else, you must be able to soldier for yourself. Be a one-man army."

_____

_____

_____

_____

_____

_____

_____

_____

DAY 38

"Part of learning to fly is learning what weighs you down. Be effective, and aware of what boosts you, and what holds you back."

_____

_____

_____

_____

_____

_____

_____

_____

DAY 39

"Life will happen. Do what you can to increase the probabilities in your favour. Always be moving. Always be advancing."

_____

_____

_____

_____

_____

_____

_____

_____

DAY 40

"Dedicate time for you. Surprise yourself. Treat yourself. Value yourself. Most importantly, love yourself."

_____

_____

_____

_____

_____

_____

_____

_____

DAY 41

"Find your inner amazing."

_____

_____

_____

_____

_____

_____

_____

_____

DAY 42

"We are meant to overcome hurdles....
and then find more to overcome."

_____

_____

_____

_____

_____

_____

_____

_____

DAY 43

"We are all born with gifts, each unique and each our own. Recognise them, use them, work them, grow them, master them."

_____

_____

_____

_____

_____

_____

_____

_____

DAY 44

"What good is a mind if it is never challenged?"

_____

_____

_____

_____

_____

_____

_____

_____

DAY 45

"Create balance! Do not wait for it to arrive!"

DAY 46

"Take the time to not only see, but also to examine."

DAY 47

"Explore your world."

DAY 48

"Don't get paralyzed by lies."

_____

_____

_____

_____

_____

_____

_____

_____

DAY 49

"Each time, a little further, a little faster,
slowly but surely, become a master."

_____

_____

_____

_____

_____

_____

_____

_____

_____

DAY 50

"Finding the balance between leveraging and centralizing your energy is paramount."

_____

_____

_____

_____

_____

_____

_____

_____

DAY 51

"Create your own inspiration."

_____

_____

_____

_____

_____

_____

_____

_____

DAY 52

"Like putting a broken bone back into place, aligning yourself can be painful, though beneficial in the long run. Short term pain, long term gain. Keep pushing it!"

_____

_____

_____

_____

_____

_____

_____

_____

DAY 53

"Find ways to calibrate with precision."

_____

_____

_____

_____

_____

_____

_____

_____

DAY 54

"Make advancements with purpose.
Always move forward; always grow with
positive momentum and direction."

_____

_____

_____

_____

_____

_____

_____

_____

DAY 55

"Levels of growth accompany levels of trials."

_____

_____

_____

_____

_____

_____

_____

_____

DAY 56

"The power of choice...learn it."

_____

_____

_____

_____

_____

_____

_____

_____

DAY 57

"When you do things for yourself,
you'll always come out on top."

DAY 58

"There is no denying it. Strength in unity."

_____

_____

_____

_____

_____

_____

_____

_____

DAY 59

"Nature has a way of natural succession."

_____

_____

_____

_____

_____

_____

_____

_____

DAY 60

"Three energies exist in our system. Energies that suck yours, energies that flow to you, and energies that work with yours to amplify and increase in power."

_____

_____

_____

_____

_____

_____

_____

_____

DAY 61

"Dreams are free and unlimited. Dream away!"

DAY 62

"Life will present you with two options.
You will either explore...or ignore."

_____

_____

_____

_____

_____

_____

_____

_____

DAY 63

"Aligning yourself with great people is better than attending any university."

_____

_____

_____

_____

_____

_____

_____

_____

_____

DAY 64

"In all that you do...act with caution, be courteous, and move with conviction."

_____

_____

_____

_____

_____

_____

_____

_____

_____

DAY 65

"Do not allow yourself to become consumed by political power and division. Focus on your internal potential of growth, rather than a country's illusion of choice and direction. The bigger battle is internal, not external."

DAY 66

"What was easy today may not be tomorrow. Stay on guard."

_____

_____

_____

_____

_____

_____

_____

_____

DAY 67

"Be quick to seek forgiveness, and quick to give it."

_____

_____

_____

_____

_____

_____

_____

_____

_____

DAY 68

*"How far do you have to walk down a
road… before you see where it leads?"*

_____

_____

_____

_____

_____

_____

_____

_____

DAY 69

"If you stay at a job you hate, and that makes you miserable, just for the money... it means that you have found the price of your soul."

_____

_____

_____

_____

_____

_____

_____

_____

DAY 70

"Those with foresight weather the storms coming from beyond the horizon; others will be washed away."

_____

_____

_____

_____

_____

_____

_____

_____

DAY 71

"Moments of clarity arise through moments of solidarity."

_____

_____

_____

_____

_____

_____

_____

_____

DAY 72

"Many tend to value the valueless things in life. Don't let true value pass you by."

_____

_____

_____

_____

_____

_____

_____

_____

DAY 73

"The wolf catches his prey, not by speed, but by endurance and teamwork, outsmarting his prey. Find, nurture, and release your inner wolf."

DAY 74

"In the trials of life...don't lose your warmth."

_____

_____

_____

_____

_____

_____

_____

_____

DAY 75

"Never be afraid to begin a new mountain and start at the bottom."

_____

_____

_____

_____

_____

_____

_____

_____

DAY 76

"*You can choose to either overcome fear, or succumb to it.*"

_____

_____

_____

_____

_____

_____

_____

_____

DAY 77

"Develop the tool of self-motivation."

DAY 78

"Any output can most likely be attributed to the input. Usually...hard work pays."

_____

_____

_____

_____

_____

_____

_____

_____

DAY 79

"Dreams are much better when you make them reality."

_____

_____

_____

_____

_____

_____

_____

_____

_____

DAY 80

"Having an exercise routine without a healthy diet is like trying to fan a fire with no wood."

_____

_____

_____

_____

_____

_____

_____

_____

DAY 81

"Gather and concentrate your energy on things you have the power to control, rather than things you are powerless to control."

_____

_____

_____

_____

_____

_____

_____

_____

DAY 82

"Find what feeds your soul, and feast on the good."

_____

_____

_____

_____

_____

_____

_____

_____

DAY 83

"You were born frail and weak, and you may die frail and weak...but it's up to you how you are in between. Live strong, die living."

DAY 84

*"2% knowing what to do, 98% doing it well,
and 100% trying to do it better every time."*

_____

_____

_____

_____

_____

_____

_____

_____

DAY 85

"Whether you like it or not, or are aware of it or not, symbols have meaning, and images carry more power than people give them credit for!"

_____

_____

_____

_____

_____

_____

_____

_____

DAY 86

"The key to accountability is determining whether or not you have the ability to be held accountable."

_____

_____

_____

_____

_____

_____

_____

_____

DAY 87

"A decision is never right or wrong until it has been made. Not making one at all though is worse than either option."

_____

_____

_____

_____

_____

_____

_____

_____

DAY 88

"The road to enlightenment begins with blindness."

_____

_____

_____

_____

_____

_____

_____

_____

DAY 89

"In order to overcome obstacles, you must recognize what they are."

DAY 90

"One can be in control of one's life, yet still have no direction. Seek purpose and fulfillment."

_____

_____

_____

_____

_____

_____

_____

_____

DAY 91

"Seek out those unique, pure moments of clarity."

DAY 92

"Before becoming part of the solution or part of the problem you have to recognize them both. Then you can choose."

_____

_____

_____

_____

_____

_____

_____

_____

DAY 93

"*Live through memories to create new ones.*"

_____

_____

_____

_____

_____

_____

_____

_____

DAY 94

"Grow with grace."

DAY 95

"Embrace conflict. Learning moments are everywhere."

_____

_____

_____

_____

_____

_____

_____

_____

DAY 96

"Look before you leap...but I recommend diving in."

_____

_____

_____

_____

_____

_____

_____

_____

DAY 97

"If you fear death, you fear life. Don't be afraid to live. LIVE with the fear of not really living."

DAY 98

*"Avoiding opposition will not mean opposition
will not find you. Never cease being mobile.
Always seek out what is good."*

_____

_____

_____

_____

_____

_____

_____

_____

DAY 99

"In a world where justice should be blind, justice is instead about what has the most likes, shares, and popular opinion."

_____

_____

_____

_____

_____

_____

_____

_____

DAY 100

"In the game of life, winning is irrelevant if you're playing for the wrong side. Do not allow evil to prevail, and always remember to Resonate with Love."

_____

_____

_____

_____

_____

_____

_____

_____

DAY 101

"Life mechanics—diagnose, troubleshoot, tear down, rebuild, refine, adjust, fine tune, enhance performance, and drive like you stole it!"

_____

_____

_____

_____

_____

_____

_____

_____

DAY 102

"Walls are meant to be climbed, barriers broken, limits pushed, and questions asked. Never fear forward motion."

_____

_____

_____

_____

_____

_____

_____

_____

DAY 103

"Grind for growth."

DAY 104

"You embarked upon a journey at birth. To be still, is to be dead. Always move forward!"

_____

_____

_____

_____

_____

_____

_____

_____

DAY 105

"Meditate on magnificence."

_____

_____

_____

_____

_____

_____

_____

_____

DAY 106

"Empathy can be blinding."

_____

_____

_____

_____

_____

_____

_____

_____

DAY 107

"We must continuously ask ourselves if there is any room for improvement."

DAY 108

"Your heart allows you to live, but the music that touches its depths can remind you what it's like to feel alive!"

_____

_____

_____

_____

_____

_____

_____

_____

DAY 109

"The size of your engine and its potential are useless with no fuel pump. Respect your heart, respect your fuel intake, and its ability to flow."

_____

_____

_____

_____

_____

_____

_____

_____

DAY 110

"Every day is a new chance for improvement.
Waste it or gain from it."

_____

_____

_____

_____

_____

_____

_____

_____

DAY 111

"The distraction is real. Find your focus, and align."

_____

_____

_____

_____

_____

_____

_____

_____

DAY 112

"You should have no fear in doing right."

_____

_____

_____

_____

_____

_____

_____

_____

DAY 113

"You are either a soldier for yourself, or a slave to yourself. The decision is being made for you already, if you haven't noticed."

DAY 114

"First you fix, then you refine."

_____

_____

_____

_____

_____

_____

_____

_____

DAY 115

"Healthy soul, body, mind. Be loving, caring, and kind.
Be unstoppable today, tomorrow, and all the time!"

_____

_____

_____

_____

_____

_____

_____

_____

DAY 116

"Your bare minimum should always be awesome.
Your maximum should always be moving forward."

_____

_____

_____

_____

_____

_____

_____

_____

DAY 117

*"Most battles are won mentally before
they are won physically."*

_____

_____

_____

_____

_____

_____

_____

_____

DAY 118

"One of the greatest victories you can achieve is harnessing yourself. Another is to maintain that victory."

_____

_____

_____

_____

_____

_____

_____

_____

DAY 119

"If we are always in the dark, we will never be able to focus. There is light in truth. Learn. Adjust. Focus. Execute action."

DAY 120

"Create systematic, symmetrical chaos."

_____

_____

_____

_____

_____

_____

_____

_____

DAY 121

"When you take flight, you look up not down, not behind. Just....Fly!"

_____

_____

_____

_____

_____

_____

_____

_____

DAY 122

"Other people's mistakes can be used for your gain. A good chess match can be won by catching the first error of the game."

_____

_____

_____

_____

_____

_____

_____

_____

DAY 123

"Sweat your stress away."

_____

_____

_____

_____

_____

_____

_____

_____

DAY 124

*"On your deathbed... do you want regrets or
experiences...or the regret of never creating them?
Ultimately, your life is yours. Nobody else's. Make
experiences, whether they turn out to be mistakes or not,
for you'll never truly know until you create them."*

DAY 125

*"What's the point of having options if you
never explore them? Go explore."*

_____

_____

_____

_____

_____

_____

_____

_____

DAY 126

"Time is of no value when you race against yourself.
Just keep running forward fast and remember to flow."

_____

_____

_____

_____

_____

_____

_____

_____

DAY 127

"Don't allow power to blind precision."

_____

_____

_____

_____

_____

_____

_____

_____

DAY 128

"Continue reaching for new potentials."

_____

_____

_____

_____

_____

_____

_____

_____

DAY 129

---

*"Small increments of awesomeness become
large increments of spectacular."*

DAY 130

"Your weaknesses control you. Overcome your weaknesses and you will truly control your life."

_____

_____

_____

_____

_____

_____

_____

_____

DAY 131

"The world owes you nothing. We all start out with a hand of cards. Play it safe or gamble. No one starts out with the same hand. Crying to the dealer won't help. Play well friends, or fold."

_____

_____

_____

_____

_____

_____

_____

_____

DAY 132

"There is nothing that can surpass the efficiency of small, precise growth on a strong foundation."

DAY 133

"The glorious pain of progress is an unmatched feeling. Embrace it."

_____

_____

_____

_____

_____

_____

_____

_____

DAY 134

"Death is something we must all eventually face and overcome, in order to get the most from life."

_____

_____

_____

_____

_____

_____

_____

_____

DAY 135

"Do not grow accustomed to the trap of hesitation.
Rather, make haste, for time never waits."

DAY 136

"Keep reminding yourself: just a little more each day."

DAY 137

"Begin to focus not on what's in front of you, but adjust and see, focus on what lies behind."

_____

_____

_____

_____

_____

_____

_____

_____

DAY 138

"Strive to thrive. The time to grow is always."

_____

_____

_____

_____

_____

_____

_____

_____

_____

DAY 139

"Begin today to fight for tomorrow."

_____

_____

_____

_____

_____

_____

_____

_____

_____

DAY 140

"I would rather move consistently forward and inconsistently backward, than consistently backward and inconsistently forward."

DAY 141

"Take in more, take in all. Filter and strain!
Remove the stain and keep the gain!"

DAY 142

"It's a give or take kind of world. It is always up to you to decide what you allow to occur, to the best of your abilities."

_____

_____

_____

_____

_____

_____

_____

_____

DAY 143

"Whatever you want to find.... there it is, inside you!"

DAY 144

"There are no repeats of yesterday. Look to tomorrow to grow again, and flow as you need to."

_____

_____

_____

_____

_____

_____

_____

_____

DAY 145

"Guide your sail where there is most wind. Don't lose energy battling unseen forces against you."

_____

_____

_____

_____

_____

_____

_____

_____

DAY 146

"From fuel, to feel, to forward action. Your body is yours and yours alone. Feed it well. Cultivate mastery!"

DAY 147

"Give credence to how far you've travelled, not how far you have to go. A journey is filled with countless variables."

_____

_____

_____

_____

_____

_____

_____

_____

_____

DAY 148

"There can only be one you. Don't exhaust yourself trying to be someone else. Be the best you!"

_____

_____

_____

_____

_____

_____

_____

_____

DAY 149

"What do you live for? What do you love for?"

DAY 150

"Leaps and bounds start with a step."

_____

_____

_____

_____

_____

_____

_____

_____

DAY 151

"Don't wonder; discover."

_____

_____

_____

_____

_____

_____

_____

_____

DAY 152

"Absorb the pain and make it your strength. Use it as a guiding light when the path darkens once again."

DAY 153

"Demolish your goals as you rush past them, and always look forward to crush new ones!"

_____

_____

_____

_____

_____

_____

_____

_____

DAY 154

"Only weakness is intimidated by confidence. Do NOT be deterred in your quest for growth."

_____

_____

_____

_____

_____

_____

_____

_____

DAY 155

"There is always a bigger picture. If you choose to devote time to look, you will see."

_____

_____

_____

_____

_____

_____

_____

_____

DAY 156

"Do not occupy yourself with things that are meant to preoccupy you. Become intentional in developing a resistance to swerving away from purpose."

DAY 157

"Don't ever forget the path you've walked. Look behind, not to travel back, but to remember accomplishments."

_____

_____

_____

_____

_____

_____

_____

_____

DAY 158

"Don't allow others to dictate your life. Rather allow love, kindness, and justice to dictate your path!"

_____

_____

_____

_____

_____

_____

_____

_____

DAY 159

"Unleash the killer of kindness within you."

_____

_____

_____

_____

_____

_____

_____

_____

DAY 160

"Rarely does one correct an error without realizing there was one."

_____

_____

_____

_____

_____

_____

_____

_____

DAY 161

*"Food feeds the stomach; knowledge feeds the mind.
Have you discovered what feeds your soul?"*

DAY 162

"Your personal best should be every tomorrow."

_____

_____

_____

_____

_____

_____

_____

_____

DAY 163

———

"Become unstoppable."

_____

_____

_____

_____

_____

_____

_____

_____

DAY 164

"Find someone that encourages stimulation of progress through mutual challenges for advancement. And be that someone!"

DAY 165

"Incentivize yourself for growth."

DAY 166

"Grow, cut, refine, shine, repeat."

_____

_____

_____

_____

_____

_____

_____

_____

DAY 167

"Easy to say, difficult to do, worthwhile to follow through."

_____

_____

_____

_____

_____

_____

_____

_____

DAY 168

"True power comes from stepping back and moving forward. Massive progression from minor regression."

_____

_____

_____

_____

_____

_____

_____

_____

DAY 169

———

"You do not need to scoop the whole lake
to get a drink of refreshing water."

_____

_____

_____

_____

_____

_____

_____

_____

_____

DAY 170

"Strive to reach peak functionality, not peak vanity. Longevity, strength, growth!"

_____

_____

_____

_____

_____

_____

_____

_____

DAY 171

"There are times when 'wait and see' is the best option. Don't discount patience during hardship."

_____

_____

_____

_____

_____

_____

_____

_____

DAY 172

"There exists a beauty unseen, always waiting to be found. Just look and see."

_____

_____

_____

_____

_____

_____

_____

_____

DAY 173

"To make the best of a day, start it at the beginning."

_____

_____

_____

_____

_____

_____

_____

_____

DAY 174

"Never deviate from constant discovery."

_____

_____

_____

_____

_____

_____

_____

_____

DAY 175

"Plan for the future using the past as a guide."

DAY 176

"Every day, do your best to be your best."

_____

_____

_____

_____

_____

_____

_____

_____

DAY 177

*"Truth and humility are very well-acquainted.
Befriend one and you befriend the other."*

DAY 178

"Identify the difference between good results and excellent results, and you will never lack in exceptionality."

_____

_____

_____

_____

_____

_____

_____

_____

DAY 179

"Be realistic about your short-term goals, and your long-term goals will be achievable dreams."

_____

_____

_____

_____

_____

_____

_____

DAY 180

"We are born with a soul of capabilities and abilities. Will you subdue it? Or will you fan its potential to a roaring flame?"

_____

_____

_____

_____

_____

_____

_____

_____

DAY 181

"Your body does not need a lot of food, rather the "right" foods to keep the motor running top-notch! Stay fit!"

DAY 182

"To lead is good, although following an excellent leader can be just as rewarding, or better."

_____

_____

_____

_____

_____

_____

_____

_____

_____

DAY 183

"The deeper you dig in yourself for discipline, the less you have to dig each time you search for it."

_____

_____

_____

_____

_____

_____

_____

_____

DAY 184

"Never forget your many qualities that make you magnificent. Now, reach for others that you haven't discovered yet."

_____

_____

_____

_____

_____

_____

_____

_____

_____

DAY 185

"Everything you do is preparation for what you will do."

_____

_____

_____

_____

_____

_____

_____

_____

DAY 186

"Ignite your insight, and flow forward."

DAY 187

"Life's not about looking good. It's about being good.
For yourself. For others. In all that you do! SHINE!"

_____

_____

_____

_____

_____

_____

_____

_____

_____

DAY 188

"In all that you do, in all your works, search for sources."

_____

_____

_____

_____

_____

_____

_____

_____

DAY 189

"Don't let the horizon determine how far to travel."

DAY 190

"Analyze, prioritize, and appreciate your own time."

DAY 191

"The secret to a long life is to try not to shorten it."

_____

_____

_____

_____

_____

_____

_____

_____

DAY 192

"Truth is often released over time. There are no chains strong enough to bind truth. It will always eventually see the light."

_____

_____

_____

_____

_____

_____

_____

_____

DAY 193

"Control your breathing! Not only will you control your life…but also the quality of it."

DAY 194

"Resilience. Let it embrace you. Embrace it. Move."

DAY 195

"Be still. Be quiet. Focus. Observe."

DAY 196

"By becoming a hero for many, you will become an enemy for others."

_____

_____

_____

_____

_____

_____

_____

_____

_____

DAY 197

"There is always someone faster and stronger...that person is you."

_____

_____

_____

_____

_____

_____

_____

_____

_____

DAY 198

"There are only two things in life you need to remember: Don't stop, and Keep moving forward."

DAY 199

"The challenge of a race is to keep a rhythmic pace. Without it you will not achieve. Strive to create harmonic advancement."

DAY 200

"The stronger the truth, the more it hurts, and sometimes the harder it is to believe."

_____

_____

_____

_____

_____

_____

_____

_____

DAY 201

"Never allow your determination to become dormant."

DAY 202

"Let your motivation for growth drive you."

_____

_____

_____

_____

_____

_____

_____

_____

DAY 203

"Differentiating between wants and needs has become an art."

_____

_____

_____

_____

_____

_____

_____

_____

DAY 204

"One of my greatest accomplishments was to give up the blatant brainwashing of television."

_____

_____

_____

_____

_____

_____

_____

_____

DAY 205

*"Make the effort to think critically for
yourself an utmost priority."*

_____

_____

_____

_____

_____

_____

_____

_____

DAY 206

*"The world can be a cruel place, but you...
you can exert the compassion it lacks."*

_____

_____

_____

_____

_____

_____

_____

_____

DAY 207

"The power is in you to control how the outside world affects you. If you don't control it, it will control you!"

_____

_____

_____

_____

_____

_____

_____

_____

DAY 208

"You must first realize that you are on a leash before you are able to remove it."

_____

_____

_____

_____

_____

_____

_____

_____

DAY 209

"There are plenty of small stars in your life that will brighten your path until the sun returns."

_____

_____

_____

_____

_____

_____

_____

_____

DAY 210

"*The willpower of one can change the will of many.*"

_____

_____

_____

_____

_____

_____

_____

_____

DAY 211

"To you, the most amazing person in the world should always be yourself."

_____

_____

_____

_____

_____

_____

_____

_____

DAY 212

"How do you change the moving tides of a raging ocean? Simply go with the flow, stay afloat, and hydrate yourself with fresh water."

DAY 213

"There's a lesson to be learned in everything."

_____

_____

_____

_____

_____

_____

_____

_____

DAY 214

"Extrapolate what you can, with whatever you can, and continue to improve. Always!"

_____

_____

_____

_____

_____

_____

_____

_____

DAY 215

"Improvement comes in many shapes and forms. It is key to recognise when it occurs, and flow with it."

DAY 216

"Do not be free of form. Rather, form freely."

DAY 217

"Consistency of kindness unconsciously creates an endless ripple of positive reciprocity. It's worth the effort."

DAY 218

"There's nothing like salt and sun in your eyes! Enjoy this life of light."

_____

_____

_____

_____

_____

_____

_____

_____

DAY 219

"We are all managers in our lives, accountable to ourselves, and serving ourselves."

_____

_____

_____

_____

_____

_____

_____

_____

DAY 220

*"If you envision something in the future,
you are preparing to create memories for it
in the past. All that's left is to live it."*

_____

_____

_____

_____

_____

_____

_____

_____

DAY 221

"There is truth in silence."

_____

_____

_____

_____

_____

_____

_____

_____

DAY 222

"The selfie generation. Never before has a generation looked so much at themselves, and never before has a generation been so blind to who they are."

_____

_____

_____

_____

_____

_____

_____

_____

_____

DAY 223

*"The most powerful voice in the world
is the silent one inside you."*

_____

_____

_____

_____

_____

_____

_____

_____

DAY 224

"We all journey to an eventual parting from this life, so we must think clearly throughout our time here about what exactly we will choose to leave behind."

DAY 225

"Educational institutions have dissolved into laughable, sad, sheep factories. Take the good, leave the bad, and question everything."

DAY 226

*"It's beautiful to create. When was the
last time you created something?"*

_____

_____

_____

_____

_____

_____

_____

_____

DAY 227

———

"The path of enlightenment tends to begin in darkness."

————————————

————————————

————————————

————————————

————————————

————————————

————————————

————————————

DAY 228

"We can manipulate, harness, and use electricity...but have you harnessed and mastered your own energy to your benefit?"

_____

_____

_____

_____

_____

_____

_____

_____

DAY 229

"Molt! Shed old skin, grow a new and improved you!"

_____

_____

_____

_____

_____

_____

_____

_____

DAY 230

"Make your journeys unforgettable."

_____

_____

_____

_____

_____

_____

_____

_____

DAY 231

"Never underestimate the power of consistency."

DAY 232

"Deviate from distraction and amplify attraction.
Let the power of positivity draw you."

_____

_____

_____

_____

_____

_____

_____

_____

DAY 233

"All we have to live for is memories.
Make them positive."

_____

_____

_____

_____

_____

_____

_____

_____

DAY 234

"Friendships are free. Having enemies comes at a price."

_____

_____

_____

_____

_____

_____

_____

_____

DAY 235

"To question is to self-water your growth."

_____

_____

_____

_____

_____

_____

_____

_____

DAY 236

*"It's not just about how far you've traveled...
but also what you've traveled through, that
gives you your unique experience."*

DAY 237

———

*"How can future generations handle problems
if we are teaching them to avoid them?"*

_____

_____

_____

_____

_____

_____

_____

_____

DAY 238

"Don't go down without a fight! Fight to get up if you're down, and fight to fly if you're standing!"

_____

_____

_____

_____

_____

_____

_____

_____

DAY 239

"Don't just teach.... inspire!"

_____

_____

_____

_____

_____

_____

_____

_____

DAY 240

———

"Be true; be you."

_____

_____

_____

_____

_____

_____

_____

_____

DAY 241

"Resistance spurs growth."

_____

_____

_____

_____

_____

_____

_____

_____

DAY 242

"The world is vast. Knowledge is left to be discovered everywhere. Fly freely without remorse."

_____

_____

_____

_____

_____

_____

_____

_____

_____

DAY 243

"Obtain knowledge. Then act and build on it."

_____

_____

_____

_____

_____

_____

_____

_____

DAY 244

"I'll take being under the sun over being under a spotlight, any day and everyday."

DAY 245

"Make precision decisions."

DAY 246

*"Size may mean strength, but lighter is mightier.
Be quick with power and slow to use it."*

DAY 247

"Gluttony comes in many shapes. Striving for simplicity, surprisingly, will produce more."

DAY 248

"Primary objective: focus. Secondary objective: understand. Then plan. Then attack. Then review. Understand. Grow. Adjust. Repeat!"

_____

_____

_____

_____

_____

_____

_____

_____

DAY 249

"You are a by-product of your decisions, and you may never know if they were good or bad until years later."

_____

_____

_____

_____

_____

_____

_____

_____

DAY 250

"Reflect on different perspectives. What falls... sometimes just floats."

_____

_____

_____

_____

_____

_____

_____

_____

DAY 251

"True intelligence is true beauty."

_____

_____

_____

_____

_____

_____

_____

_____

DAY 252

"Friends inspire, enemies conspire."

DAY 253

"The world is amazing when you spread kindness. Both kindness and contacts; create, make, and keep them."

DAY 254

"When it comes to helping others: If you can and are able, do. I once was a 'can and able but won't.'. I'm glad I changed."

DAY 255

"Simple words from simple people can have a complex impact. Never be shy to lend an ear or strike up a conversation."

DAY 256

"Share food and break bread. Invite and enjoy the company of others."

_____

_____

_____

_____

_____

_____

_____

_____

DAY 257

"There is beauty in everything. Search for it and see."

_____

_____

_____

_____

_____

_____

_____

_____

DAY 258

"You will never achieve if you never trek."

DAY 259

"You may not be able to help the whole world...but you can easily help individuals. Give freely from the heart."

_____

_____

_____

_____

_____

_____

_____

_____

DAY 260

"There are forces that exist that want you to fly... just as others want you to sink. Continue to reach... and you shall be pulled."

_____

_____

_____

_____

_____

_____

_____

_____

DAY 261

"Challenge yourself for change."

_____

_____

_____

_____

_____

_____

_____

_____

DAY 262

"It is unreasonable to try to reason with those who do not know the meaning of the word."

_____

_____

_____

_____

_____

_____

_____

_____

DAY 263

"The harder it is, the easier it gets."

DAY 264

"I would rather live in a world, lawless, but with love and gratitude, than in a world with laws, and a lack of love and empathy."

_____

_____

_____

_____

_____

_____

_____

_____

DAY 265

"Once you have the wants in life, you realize it's not what you need. Appreciate and strive for the real needs in life."

_____

_____

_____

_____

_____

_____

_____

_____

_____

DAY 266

"Life speaks; learn to listen to the signs."

_____

_____

_____

_____

_____

_____

_____

_____

DAY 267

"Health never rests."

_____

_____

_____

_____

_____

_____

_____

_____

_____

DAY 268

"The motor for your mind is your heart. Protect it, feed it well, keep it clean, and all that passes through it, filter."

_____

_____

_____

_____

_____

_____

_____

_____

DAY 269

"Hydrate your mind with the water of knowledge."

_____

_____

_____

_____

_____

_____

_____

_____

DAY 270

*"Work up a momentum of steady achievement,
then maintain a state of steady progression."*

_____

_____

_____

_____

_____

_____

_____

_____

DAY 271

"The entrapment of vanity will enslave many. What is a body without a mind?"

_____

_____

_____

_____

_____

_____

_____

_____

DAY 272

*"The answers to questions not yet understood
are everywhere around us."*

DAY 273

"Birth through water; death by dust. Stay hydrated with the life source!"

_____

_____

_____

_____

_____

_____

_____

_____

DAY 274

"Manufactured obsolescence is not just with products."

_____

_____

_____

_____

_____

_____

_____

_____

DAY 275

"Unfortunately, arrogance and ignorance flow in abundance in this system of things. Maneuver around it, freely and safely."

_____

_____

_____

_____

_____

_____

_____

_____

_____

DAY 276

"A strong foundation for life is to exert love and gratitude."

_____

_____

_____

_____

_____

_____

_____

_____

DAY 277

"Be aware. Tolerance to the intolerant is weakness."

_____

_____

_____

_____

_____

_____

_____

_____

DAY 278

"Truth cannot be destroyed... only hidden."

_____

_____

_____

_____

_____

_____

_____

_____

DAY 279

"Don't you EVER give up on you."

_____

_____

_____

_____

_____

_____

_____

_____

_____

DAY 280

"Find ways to replace the word 'hate' in your vocabulary."

DAY 281

"The world and all its inner workings are nothing but a cheap parlour trick."

_____

_____

_____

_____

_____

_____

_____

_____

DAY 282

"Life unravels an interesting winding road...
yet it's always straight as an arrow."

_____

_____

_____

_____

_____

_____

_____

_____

DAY 283

"Eliminate resistance when in flight."

DAY 284

"Until death, everything is life. Live it with vitality."

DAY 285

"Believe nothing of what you hear and half of what you see. Do not fear to investigate for the truth."

DAY 286

"We are born fragile, but live strong, powerful, and with vigour. Be determined to avoid frailty."

_____

_____

_____

_____

_____

_____

_____

_____

_____

DAY 287

"Just remember, you own nothing but what's in you."

_____

_____

_____

_____

_____

_____

_____

_____

DAY 288

"It is not by your ability to do or not do, rather, it is by your efforts to achieve, that you can judge yourself."

_____

_____

_____

_____

_____

_____

_____

_____

DAY 289

"Sweat soothes the soul."

_____

_____

_____

_____

_____

_____

_____

_____

_____

DAY 290

"Some days are hard, bleak, dark… but… they ARE STILL days of life that we live and learn from. Love each breath you take, and don't take your breath away."

_____

_____

_____

_____

_____

_____

_____

_____

DAY 291

"Absorb all that is light, and reflect. Become bright."

_____

_____

_____

_____

_____

_____

_____

_____

DAY 292

"Honesty creates certainty."

DAY 293

"If you cannot divide and conquer.... then just conquer and don't waste time with dividing."

DAY 294

"Fractalize your workouts."

_____

_____

_____

_____

_____

_____

_____

_____

DAY 295

"Do not fear taking back what was once yours."

DAY 296

*"Intelligence is hard to hide, though
easy to mimic. Don't be fooled."*

_____

_____

_____

_____

_____

_____

_____

_____

_____

DAY 297

"Unity makes force; division creates weakness."

_____

_____

_____

_____

_____

_____

_____

_____

DAY 298

"Big and strong will almost always be trumped by fast and efficient."

DAY 299

"Meditation of the mind is time well spent...
meditation on your soul... is eternal."

_____

_____

_____

_____

_____

_____

_____

DAY 300

"Sustainability, flexibility, strength, longevity, preventive maintenance, controlled growth, glow... go get it!"

_____

_____

_____

_____

_____

_____

_____

_____

DAY 301

"These new generations are growing accustomed to looking down for directions when above us are signs from old. Look up."

DAY 302

*"Enjoy your journey; you only have one,
and where it ends is not up to you. So,
make it the best, and be the best."*

_____

_____

_____

_____

_____

_____

_____

_____

DAY 303

"Don't fall into traps written by men who build their own walls."

_____

_____

_____

_____

_____

_____

_____

_____

DAY 304

"In its simplest form, everything is just a matter of time."

DAY 305

"Prevent yourself from the act of continuous negativity. Do not reciprocate hate."

DAY 306

"Once you embrace uncertainty, all that remains is certainty."

DAY 307

*"The best music is the performance that's never recorded.
Not everything needs to be captured for enjoyment!"*

_____

_____

_____

_____

_____

_____

_____

_____

DAY 308

"To get where you want to go, you may have to change who you are. However, after some thought, you may change where you want to go."

_____

_____

_____

_____

_____

_____

_____

_____

DAY 309

*"What good is a paradise if there is
no one to share it with?"*

_____

_____

_____

_____

_____

_____

_____

_____

DAY 310

"The art of empathy is learned by few, and some replace that art with judgement and ego. Reject these. Practice true art."

DAY 311

"Traverse through the hues of life with divine fluidity."

DAY 312

"There is no benefit to rebelling against truth and light."

_____

_____

_____

_____

_____

_____

_____

_____

DAY 313

"Recognize the difference between practical and radical."

_____

_____

_____

_____

_____

_____

_____

_____

DAY 314

"Is there a battle between the mind and body? Learn that they are one and the same. Control your mind, and you control your body."

DAY 315

"Search for enlightenment."

_____

_____

_____

_____

_____

_____

_____

_____

DAY 316

"*Today, try to bring brightness into the worlds of others. Repeat daily.*"

_____

_____

_____

_____

_____

_____

_____

_____

DAY 317

"Work on doing good, and do good work."

_____

_____

_____

_____

_____

_____

_____

_____

DAY 318

"Become a light worker."

_____

_____

_____

_____

_____

_____

_____

_____

DAY 319

"One degree off course, and your distance from your path increases over time if it is not corrected. Fly straight, my friends. On target. Ever growing."

DAY 320

"Hear behind the silence, and you will hear music."

_____

_____

_____

_____

_____

_____

_____

_____

DAY 321

"Meet, greet, give light."

_____

_____

_____

_____

_____

_____

_____

_____

DAY 322

"Free is not always good, and what is good is rarely free. There is a price for everything."

_____

_____

_____

_____

_____

_____

_____

_____

DAY 323

*"Search for conversation, but most importantly, know
when to stay and listen, and know when to leave."*

DAY 324

"Eyes are the window to the soul, but it's a smile that invites you to look in them."

_____

_____

_____

_____

_____

_____

_____

_____

DAY 325

———

"A path can be illuminated by sun or moon.
Travel forward in any light, day or night."

———————————————————————

———————————————————————

———————————————————————

———————————————————————

———————————————————————

———————————————————————

———————————————————————

———————————————————————

———————————————————————

DAY 326

"The hues of colour in life are layers deep. Search behind for the source of that seen in the foreground."

_____

_____

_____

_____

_____

_____

_____

_____

DAY 327

"You cannot flame a fire that was completely put out yesterday. Start fresh. Past is past. Light a new fire today."

DAY 328

"Work will reveal reward, though it may not be revealed at the time you want it to be."

DAY 329

"Chase the sunset and it will never go dark again."

DAY 330

"A compilation of random acts of kindness will create a book of life with marvelous adventures and memories."

_____

_____

_____

_____

_____

_____

_____

_____

DAY 331

"The sooner you begin to love, the sooner you begin to really live."

_____

_____

_____

_____

_____

_____

_____

_____

DAY 332

"The time of awakening will be a revelation of revelations."

_____

_____

_____

_____

_____

_____

_____

_____

DAY 333

"Create a thirst of curiosity and quench it with wisdom. Seek clean, pure water."

DAY 334

"Make yourself unforgettable."

_____

_____

_____

_____

_____

_____

_____

_____

DAY 335

"Arrogance and ignorance may get you to some places, but not far, and not for long. You can't fake it forever."

_____

_____

_____

_____

_____

_____

_____

_____

DAY 336

"Do not allow yourself to become a slave to bad habits."

_____

_____

_____

_____

_____

_____

_____

_____

DAY 337

"If knowledge is not shared, it is wasted."

_____

_____

_____

_____

_____

_____

_____

_____

DAY 338

"Small resistance in a wire prevents efficient flow. So too, small negative walls in life prevent progressive travels!"

_____

_____

_____

_____

_____

_____

_____

_____

DAY 339

"It is in darkness where true forms come to light. Remember your days of sun, and recall them to see clearly."

_____

_____

_____

_____

_____

_____

_____

_____

DAY 340

"In this day and age, it's kill with kindness, or be killed for being kind. Will you stand for something you believe in, even if it means pain? Will you stand for truth?"

_____

_____

_____

_____

_____

_____

_____

_____

_____

DAY 341

"Calibrate yourself."

_____

_____

_____

_____

_____

_____

_____

_____

DAY 342

"At what point does a pig become a wolf, and a wolf become a pig?"

_____

_____

_____

_____

_____

_____

_____

_____

DAY 343

"Seek enhancement in all you do."

DAY 344

"Generations of indoctrination evolve into accepted tradition. Question everything."

DAY 345

"Sometimes poison tastes delicious. Be careful what you consume!"

_____

_____

_____

_____

_____

_____

_____

_____

DAY 346

"Learn to learn again."

_____

_____

_____

_____

_____

_____

_____

_____

DAY 347

"Incorporate a rejuvenation cycle of your mind intermittently throughout life."

DAY 348

"What's the one thing you would teach your younger self—what if you could go back in time and say only one thing?"

_____

_____

_____

_____

_____

_____

_____

_____

_____

DAY 349

"Hydrate with life."

DAY 350

"There's a great sigh of relief when a danger averts itself. Let it do so."

_____

_____

_____

_____

_____

_____

_____

_____

_____

DAY 351

"You shouldn't judge a book by its cover, but the cover should give you a damn good idea about what's inside."

DAY 352

"It's the consistency and perseverance in the search for perfection that must linger in your mind at all times, regardless of the fact that you may never reach it."

_____

_____

_____

_____

_____

_____

_____

_____

DAY 353

*"Remember! No matter how successful you are,
no matter how much wealth you have, time can
never be bought. Spend wisely, friends!"*

DAY 354

"You, yourself, are a walking "team." There is an "I" in team! Every muscle and body part plays a role in what you do and who you are."

DAY 355

"Anyone can learn anything with time and dedication. Mastery demands certain qualities others may not possess."

DAY 356

"You are the best stock to own. Invest in yourself.
Take calculated risks for your own maximum ROI!"

DAY 357

"How do you make yourself feel, and what do you do to make yourself feel that way? Can you improve it?"

DAY 358

"Efforts do not go unnoticed. Neither does a lack of effort."

DAY 359

"Ultimately, there is no harm in overflowing
with overwhelming kindness."

_____

_____

_____

_____

_____

_____

_____

_____

_____

DAY 360

"Be exclusive."

DAY 361

"Humility-loyalty-love. These things have no limits. Indulge."

DAY 362

"Great accomplishments consists of many, many smaller ones. It is important to understand that these small accomplishments do not lack in importance."

DAY 363

"Knowledge truly equates to power, though it's a lonely journey of acquisition. Fear not to trek alone or with little company."

_____

_____

_____

_____

_____

_____

_____

_____

DAY 364

*"Give freely, but also, learn to be
open to receive from others."*

_____

_____

_____

_____

_____

_____

_____

_____

DAY 365

"Know the earth, know your soul."

_____

_____

_____

_____

_____

_____

_____

_____

_____

ONE YEAR COMPLETE

Can you believe that it's been one year since you started this book? Were there any particular days that really had an impact on you? Any moments that shifted your awareness to a new level? Did anything really stand out and captivate you? Reflect back on the year and look at all the moments that made you think differently, more in-depth, or from a different perspective. All of those moments were droplets of growth. They were fertilizer for your soul. It is those moments that, at the core, inspire change in you! It is those moments that create a natural trend of growth by exercising your thoughts in new ways.

Perhaps there was one, or more, days that really struck a chord with you. Perhaps not the exact quote itself, but the passage may have sparked new meaning or hit home in your heart. I recommend that you take those special days and highlight them. Make them your own. Work on them, and leverage them in your own way. I encourage you to begin your own journey of creating something similar that you can reflect on in the future, or even pass on to others.

I again thank you for taking the time (literally, one year of devotion) to reading this book and hopefully, as you reflect back on where you were one year ago, you are able to see a difference compared to where you are today. Enjoy your continuous journey in this wonderful world of life and I hope to have left you anxious—waiting for my next Inspirations in Book 2.

Wolfgang Schifer

ACKNOWLEDGMENTS

I would like to thank first and foremost, my sister Ingrid, who always pushes me towards new ideas, and who is secretly, but not so secretly, in a sibling competition with me, and motivates me always. I love you, Sis! I also would like to thank Marta Silvia Tabares for planting a seed for writing a book at the appropriate time, so that it sprouted at a needed time. Thank you to Rafael Vega and Alejandro Maya Toro for providing me with a precise Spanish translation for this book. Thank you to the Gem Gallery for doing a great job on my wolf necklace pendant that I wear every day. It symbolises courage and strength, and it was a constant reminder for me to finalise this accomplishment. Thanks to Cristoph Koniczek for having the patience of a saint, putting up with my questions, and helping me with the publishing process.

And lastly, thank YOU, the reader, who with your help spreading the word, will provide the means to keep me on my writing route in life. Thank you all for having a part to play in my first published book.

ADDITIONAL NOTES

ADDITIONAL NOTES

_____

_____

_____

_____

_____

_____

_____

_____

_____

_____

_____

_____

ADDITIONAL NOTES

_____

_____

_____

_____

_____

_____

_____

_____

_____

_____

_____

_____

ADDITIONAL NOTES

ADDITIONAL NOTES